D0624897

Octopuses
Clever Ocean Creatures

By Mara Grunbaum

Children's Press®
An Imprint of Scholastic Inc.

Nature's
CHILDREN

Content Consultant
Becky Ellsworth
Curator, Shores Region
Columbus Zoo and Aquarium

Library of Congress Cataloging-in-Publication Data
Names: Grunbaum, Mara, author.
Title: Octopuses: clever ocean creatures/by Mara Grunbaum.
Description: New York, NY: Children's Press, an imprint of Scholastic Inc., 2020. | Series: Nature's children | Includes index.
Identifiers: LCCN 2019004830| ISBN 9780531229927 (library binding) | ISBN 9780531239148 (paperback)
Subjects: LCSH: Octopuses—Juvenile literature.
Classification: LCC QL430.3.O2 G78 2020 | DDC 594/.56—dc23

Design by Anna Tunick Tabachnik

Creative Direction: Judith E. Christ for Scholastic

Produced by Spooky Cheetah Press

Printed in Heshan, China 62

SCHOLASTIC, CHILDREN'S PRESS, NATURE'S CHILDREN™, and associated logos
are trademarks and/or registered trademarks of Scholastic Inc.

1 2 3 4 5 6 7 8 9 10 R 29 28 27 26 25 24 23 22 21 20

Scholastic Inc., 557 Broadway, New York, NY 10012.

Photographs ©: cover: OceanBodhi/iStockphoto; 1: Don Farrall/Getty Images; 4: Jim McMahon/Mapman®; 4 leaf silo and throughout: stockgraphicdesigns.com; 5 left: NadzeyaShanchuk/Shutterstock; 5 top center: Les Perysty/Shutterstock; 5 small octopus and throughout: ioanmasay/iStockphoto; 5 bottom left: Steven Hunt/Getty Images; 7: Jeff Rotman/NPL/Minden Pictures; 8-9: Brian Pearce Photography/Alamy Images; 10: DeAgostini/DEA/Foto Thelma & Louise/Getty Images; 11: David Liittschwager/National Geographic Creative; 13: Biosphoto/Alamy Images; 14 top left: Marevision/age fotostock; 14 top right: Christian Vidal/Biosphoto; 14 bottom left: Ron Offermans/Buiten-beeld/Minden Pictures; 14 bottom right: Humberto Ramirez/Getty Images; 16-17: Jurgen Freund/Nature Picture Library; 18-19: Yusuke Yoshino/Nature Production/Minden Pictures; 20-21: Brandon Cole Marine Photography; 23: Jeff Rotman/Getty Images; 24-25: Robert Sisson/National Geographic Creative; 26-27: Jeffrey Rotman/Biosphoto/Minden Pictures; 28-29: Marevision/age fotostock; 31: Millard H. Sharp/Science Source; 32-33: Reinhard Dirscherl/ullstein bild/Getty Images; 34-35: New York Public Library/Science Source; 37: Photononstop Images/Eurasia Press/Media Bakery; 38-39: Julian Stratenschulte/picture-alliance/dpa/AP Images; 40-41: Robert Sisson/National Geographic Creative; 42 snail: Eric Isselee/Shutterstock; 42 slug: ultramarinfoto/iStockphoto; 42 clam: Andrew J. Martinez/SeaPics.com; 42 nautilus: Brandon Cole Marine Photography; 43 cuttlefish: David Doubilet/National Geographic Image Collection/Getty Images; 43 squid: Solvin Zankl/NPL/Minden Pictures; 43 common octopus: microdon/Stone/Getty Images; 46: Don Farrall/Getty Images.

◀ **Cover image shows an octopus swimming through the Pacific Ocean near Hawaii.**

Table of Contents

Fact File: Octopuses

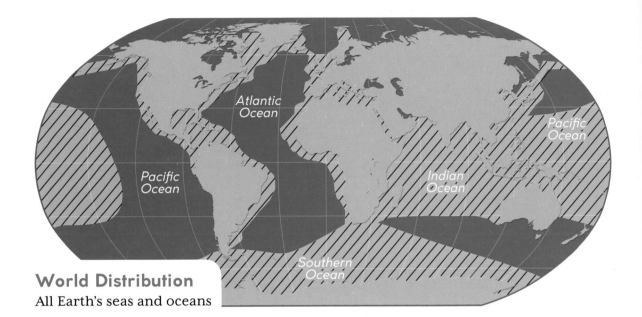

World Distribution
All Earth's seas and oceans

Habitat
Coral reefs, kelp forests, rocks, tide pools, open ocean, and the deep sea

Habits
Almost always solitary; change skin color and texture to match surroundings or to communicate; can spray ink to escape attackers

Diet
Mainly various invertebrates, such as shrimp, lobsters, crabs, snails, and clams

Distinctive Features
Soft, boneless bodies; eight arms; small heads; large, saclike mantles; suckers on arms

Fast Fact
Octopuses' blood contains copper, which makes it blue.

Size Range

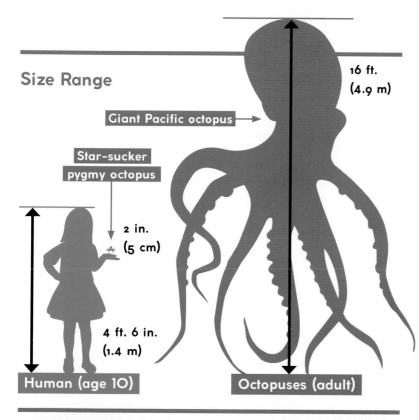

Giant Pacific octopus →

Star-sucker pygmy octopus

2 in.
(5 cm)

16 ft.
(4.9 m)

4 ft. 6 in.
(1.4 m)

Human (age 10)

Octopuses (adult)

Classification

CLASS
Cephalopoda
(octopuses, squids,
cuttlefish, and
nautiluses)

ORDER
Octopoda (octopuses)

FAMILY
13 families

GENUS
41 genera

SPECIES
300 species, including:
Enteroctopus dofleini
(giant Pacific octopus)
Octopus vulgaris
(common octopus)
Thaumoctopus mimicus
(mimic octopus)
Octopus briareus
(Caribbean reef
octopus)

◄ This day octopus
uses webbing between
its arms to catch food.

CHAPTER 1

Aliens of the Sea

A diver swims through the blue-green Pacific Ocean. Suddenly, a strange creature shoots up through the water in front of her. Two eyes appear out of nowhere. Then eight long arms spread out. This otherwordly animal is a giant Pacific octopus!

The oceans are home to about 300 **species** of octopus. They live in waters all around the world. The tiniest species, the star-sucker pygmy octopus, is smaller than a tennis ball. The largest, the giant Pacific octopus, can grow to 16 feet (4.9 meters) long.

Octopuses are some of the smartest **invertebrates** on the planet. They can change colors quickly and twist their bodies into different shapes. Some people think these habits make octopuses seem like aliens. But these strange and fascinating creatures live right here on Earth.

▶ A giant Pacific octopus can dwarf a human diver.

An Ocean of Octopuses

Octopuses are **solitary** animals. Each one finds its own place to call home. Where that is depends on the type of octopus. There are species that live on coral reefs, in kelp forests, and in the deep sea. There are even octopuses in the icy waters around Antarctica. These animals can survive temperatures as low as -2°F (-18.9°C).

Scientists know more about some octopuses than others. It's easiest to study species that live in shallow waters near shore. Finding a deep-sea octopus is much harder. Scientists have to use underwater robots to study these species, including some that glow!

All octopuses live in salt water. They can't survive in rivers or lakes. Some species can spend brief periods out of the water. They crawl onto the beach to hunt during low tide. As long as they stay moist, their skin absorbs some oxygen. But they still breathe best underwater. After a few minutes, the octopuses slip back beneath the waves.

◀ This octopus is using its muscular arms to move around on land.

Peculiar Parts

An octopus's body is made up of three main sections: the mantle, head, and arms. The animal's limbs attach directly to its head. That's why octopuses and their relatives are called cephalopods— a Greek word that means "head-feet."

The bag-like mantle is on top. It holds most of the octopus's organs, such as its gills and stomach. The mantle also contains three hearts. One central heart pumps blood through the body. Smaller hearts on either side send blood to the gills.

The octopus's head is in the middle of its body. This is where you'll find its brain, as well. The octopus's two large eyes are on the sides of its head. They give the animal excellent vision. The octopus's mouth, which is a hard beak, is at the bottom, surrounded by eight flexible arms. Each arm has two rows of strong, cuplike suckers. Tiny muscles can tighten each sucker to create an extremely strong grip.

▶ An octopus can fit its entire body through a hole big enough to fit its beak.

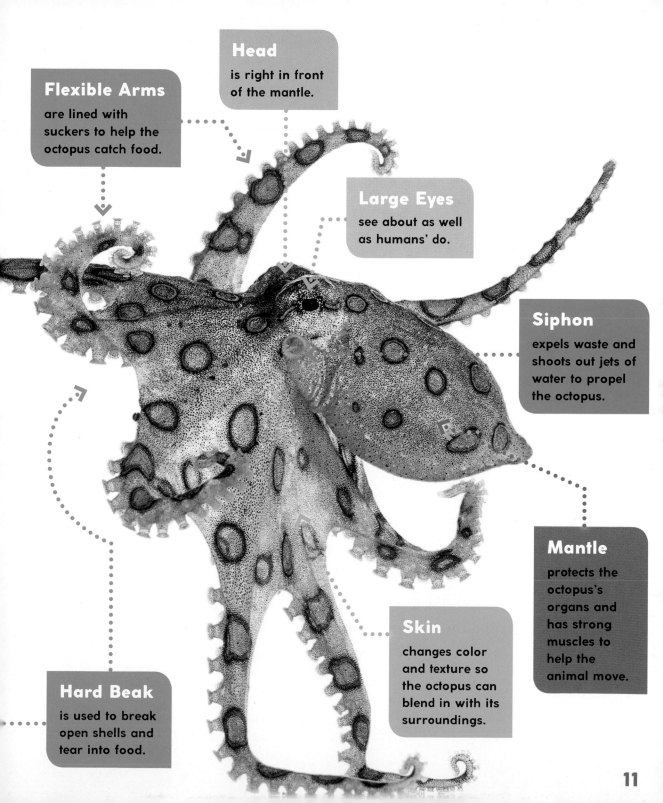

Flexible Arms
are lined with suckers to help the octopus catch food.

Head
is right in front of the mantle.

Large Eyes
see about as well as humans' do.

Siphon
expels waste and shoots out jets of water to propel the octopus.

Mantle
protects the octopus's organs and has strong muscles to help the animal move.

Skin
changes color and texture so the octopus can blend in with its surroundings.

Hard Beak
is used to break open shells and tear into food.

11

CHAPTER 2

Shape-Shifters

Unlike many invertebrates, an octopus doesn't have an **exoskeleton**. Its body is mostly muscle. In most species, the only hard part of the animal is its sharp beak. Octopuses are extremely flexible. They can squeeze into small hiding spots and reach into crevices to **forage**.

Controlling so many muscles takes coordination. An octopus's large brain keeps track of all eight arms. Each arm also has a miniature "brain" where it connects to the body. That lets the arms make some decisions on their own!

All octopuses are **carnivores**. They mostly eat invertebrates, such as shrimp, crabs, and clams. Some hunt fish or smaller octopuses. Large species can even catch small sharks and seabirds!

Most octopuses are **nocturnal**. Others are active at dawn and dusk. Though the animals have good eyesight, they don't rely on it to find food. Instead, they hunt by touch and smell.

▶ This coconut octopus has squeezed into an empty clam shell.

Crab

An octopus uses its strong suckers to immobilize a crab.

Clam

▶ An octopus's raspy tongue helps it drill through the closed shell of a clam.

Shrimp

▶ Octopuses can find shrimp to eat by lifting rocks and reaching into crevices.

Lobster

▶ An octopus can use its sharp beak to break open lobster shells.

Fast Fact
An octopus's
suckers run in two
rows down its arms.

On the Prowl

An octopus's arms are its best hunting tool.
Its suckers are extremely sensitive to touch. The octopus
crawls around and feels for hidden **prey**. One arm might
explore some seagrass while another reaches under a
rock. Many species have webbed arms. They spread the
web to trap prey inside.

The octopus's suckers also sense chemicals in the
water. That means the arms can taste what they touch.
If an arm finds something that tastes like food, it latches
on with its strong suckers. It passes the prey from one
sucker to the next. This works like a conveyor belt to bring
the food to the octopus's beak.

The octopus bites its prey and injects **venom**. This
quickly kills the animal and starts to soften the meat
inside. The octopus uses its beak, suckers, and raspy
tongue to break open crab and clam shells. It swallows
the soft meat inside and leaves the shells behind.

◀ An octopus can
eat many species
of invertebrates by
breaking their shells
with its hard beak.

Masters of Disguise

Octopuses have to be careful while they're hunting. They're **predators**, but they can also be prey. Big fish, seals, sharks, and dolphins like to eat octopuses. With no shell for protection, an octopus is easy to attack.

One way octopuses stay safe is through **camouflage**. They can blend in with their surroundings almost perfectly. Octopus skin contains packets of color called **chromatophores**. These change size to alter the color of the octopus's skin. Some species make this change in less than half a second! A species called the day octopus changes color more than 150 times an hour as it forages. Octopuses can also adjust their skin texture. This helps them match everything from rocks to seagrass.

Instead of trying to match its background, the mimic octopus does something different. It changes its body shape. It makes itself look like animals that predators find less tasty. It can imitate a flounder, a stinging jellyfish, or a sea snake!

▶ Can you spot the octopus that made its skin spiny to blend in with this reef?

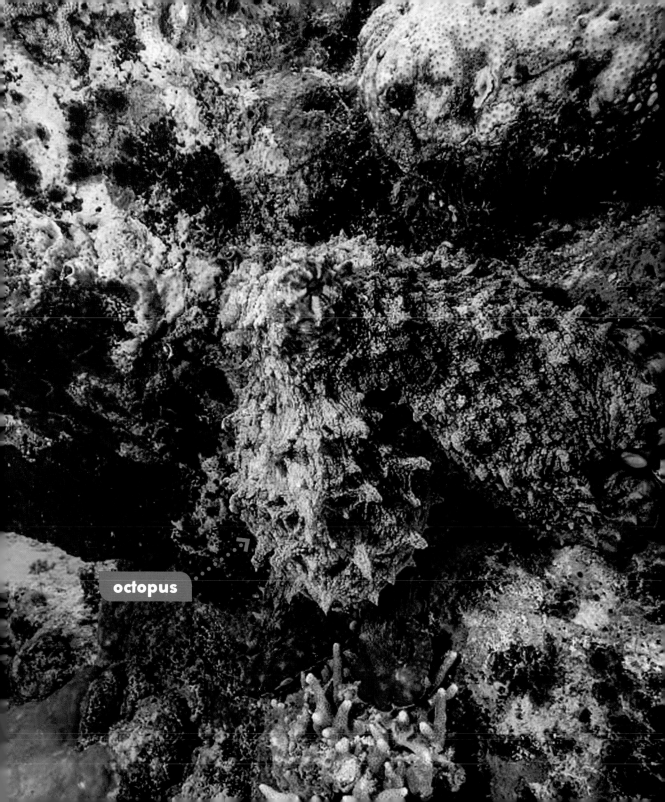

octopus

Keep Out!

When they aren't foraging, most octopuses stay hidden. They make **dens** under rocks or inside coral reefs. They may arrange pebbles and shells to cover the entrance. If another animal gets too close, the octopus shoots water from its siphon to shoo it away.

Octopuses are quick learners and good problem-solvers. They can also make dens in objects they find on the seafloor. Divers have found octopuses nesting in glass bottles, old shoes, and even shipwrecks! In Indonesia, a species called the veined octopus picks up coconut shells that fall into the water. An octopus might carry one of the shells around as it forages. Then it pulls the shell over its body to hide.

Some octopuses bring food back to their dens to eat it. Over time, a pile of shells builds up outside. But this can be a dead giveaway to predators that an octopus lives there. After about a month, the octopus moves on to another spot.

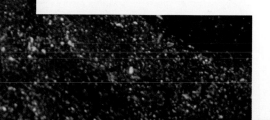

◀ Clamshells sit outside the den of the octopus that ate them.

Escape Artists

Even if hiding and shooting water from its siphons fail, the octopus has more defense options. It will do anything it can to scare and confuse predators that get too close. First, the octopus makes itself look bigger. It spreads its arms and turns a startling color, like white, blue, or red.

Many octopuses have a secret weapon. A special sac inside the mantle contains dark brown, black, or red ink. If a predator approaches, the octopus shoots the ink out of its siphon. The dark cloud blocks the predator's view. Meanwhile, the octopus jets away.

If a predator does catch an octopus, the invertebrate still has options. It might bite the attacker with its sharp beak. An octopus's arms can also detach from its body. If the predator grabs an arm, the octopus lets it go. The arm keeps wiggling to distract the predator while the octopus makes its getaway. Over the next few weeks, the missing arm grows back.

▶ A giant Pacific octopus can release enough ink to cloud a 3,000-gallon tank.

CHAPTER 3

Life and Death

Most octopuses live only a year or two.

Larger species can live for three or four. One kind of deep-sea octopus lives at least six years. No matter their lifespan, octopuses spend almost the whole time alone. There's only one time when octopuses want to meet each other. That's near the end of their lives, when they're ready to **mate**. A male and female use sight and smell to find each other. They mate quickly, and the male dies soon afterward. The female prepares to raise her eggs.

A mother octopus can lay tens of thousands of eggs at a time. She weaves them together in long strings. If she has a den, she hangs the eggs inside it. Otherwise, she simply wraps them in her arms. For the next few months, she guards the eggs around the clock to protect them from predators. She blows water over them and wipes them with her arms to keep them clean.

▶ **A coconut octopus near Indonesia carefully guards her eggs.**

eggs

Bursting Out

Octopus eggs take two to three months to develop in warm water. The **embryos** grow more slowly when it's cold. A species called the Pacific warty octopus lives in deep, chilly water. Females of that species guard their eggs for more than four years!

When most octopuses hatch, each is no bigger than a grain of rice. The babies have short, stubby arms and very few chromatophores. Other species have fewer hatchlings, but they're born bigger. Deep-sea octopuses can be more than 1.5 inches (3.8 centimeters) long when they hatch. They come out looking like miniature adults.

The whole time the eggs are developing, the octopus mother doesn't eat. She becomes smaller and weaker as the embryos grow. After her eggs hatch, she might blow one last jet of water at them to send them on their way. The mother dies soon after that. The baby octopuses are on their own.

◀ A newborn octopus escapes from its egg case.

Drifting Along

Octopuses grow up differently depending on their species. Those that are born bigger don't travel far from where they hatch. They immediately move onto the seafloor and start living as adults.

Tiny hatchlings are a different story. They start their lives as **plankton** drifting at sea. For several months, they float along with ocean currents. They eat other microscopic organisms drifting nearby. This is an extremely dangerous time for a young octopus. Many animals, from small fish to giant whales, feed on plankton. Most octopus hatchlings aren't lucky enough to make it past this stage.

The octopuses that do manage to survive grow extremely quickly. They gain about 5 percent of their body weight each day. A human newborn who grew that fast would weigh 30 pounds (13.6 kilograms) after a month! The hatchlings soon become big enough to swim against the current. Then they settle down into their adult **habitat**.

▶ A young Caribbean reef octopus is no bigger than this diver's finger.

Fast Fact
Octopuses usually switch dens every week or two.

Settling In

On the seafloor, an octopus becomes part of the **ecosystem**. It lives around hundreds or even thousands of other species. For some, the arrival of an octopus is bad news. Invertebrates such as snails and scallops might become the octopus's next meal.

Other species like having octopuses nearby. Seals and dolphins can hunt them for food. **Scavengers**, such as sea stars, pick at the remains that an octopus piles outside its den. Hermit crabs also benefit from octopus neighbors. These crabs have soft bodies. They need to find snail shells to live inside. An octopus den provides a nice pile to choose from. The shells may still be there even after the octopus has moved on.

An octopus creates several of these habitats in its lifetime. But after a few years, it stops finding new spots. Instead, an octopus gets ready to build its last den. It's time to mate and begin the cycle again.

◀ These common octopuses live on a reef near Spain.

CHAPTER 4

A Secret History

In 2009, a group of scientists made a shocking announcement. They had found three octopus **fossils** in ancient rocks in Lebanon. The fossils looked similar to modern octopuses, but they were almost 100 million years old.

Finding a complete octopus fossil is almost impossible. After an octopus dies, scavengers usually eat its body. If the dead octopus is not eaten, its soft body rots quickly. There's nothing left except the hard beak.

Scientists think the fossil octopuses fell on a part of the seafloor with no scavengers. Then layers of sand quickly washed over the bodies before they could decay. This preserved the octopuses' arms, suckers, and even ink sacs.

Scientists still don't know everything about ancient octopuses. But they'll keep working to uncover even more about these mysterious creatures.

▶ **This remarkably detailed octopus fossil was found in France in 1982.**

Squishy Similarities

Although the origin of octopuses is largely mysterious, scientists know more about the family of animals they come from. Octopuses are closely related to other cephalopods, including nautiluses, cuttlefish, and squid.

The **ancestors** of cephalopods had spiral shells. Scientists have discovered fossils of these shells from 490 million years ago. That's before there were **mammals**, birds, or any other animals on land.

Today, the only cephalopods with these spiral shells are nautiluses. Their shells cover most of their bodies. They shoot water out of the shell's opening to swim. Squid and cuttlefish don't have shells. Cuttlefish use camouflage for protection. Squid rely mostly on speed.

The giant squid is the largest cephalopod on the planet. It can measure at least 40 ft. (12.2 m) long and weigh nearly 2,000 lb. (907.2 kg). These enormous animals live very deep in the ocean. Despite their size, no one had ever spotted a giant squid in its natural habitat until 2012!

◀ Nautiluses have up to 90 suckerless tentacles.

Myths and Mysteries

Octopuses and their relatives have long been the subject of legend. As early as the 1100s, Norwegian sailors thought they saw monsters at sea. For centuries, they told stories about the kraken. They said this huge monster had many long arms and could pull a whole ship underwater. Then it would eat the unfortunate crew.

Scientists now believe these myths were based on cephalopods. Sailors had probably seen animals such as the giant squid or giant Pacific octopus. Because the sailors didn't know anything about the animals, they made up stories. The kraken and other sea monsters still appear in movies today.

Most people now know that cephalopods aren't monsters. But there are still many mysteries about them. In 2016, scientists discovered a new octopus species in deep water near Hawaii. It had pale skin and was almost see-through. Many people who saw a video of the creature thought it looked like an underwater ghost.

▶ This painting from the 1700s shows "the kraken" attacking a ship.

CHAPTER 5

Octopuses and Humans

Despite the myths, most octopuses aren't dangerous to people. They usually want to stay hidden and keep to themselves.

Only blue-ringed octopuses have venom that is deadly to people. Though their bodies are small—about 2 in. (5.1 cm) long—they have a bite that can kill an adult human. But the animals only bite if they're attacked or stepped on. They don't go out of their way to hurt anyone.

Humans do hunt octopuses, though. People around the world, from the United States to Japan, eat octopus meat. About 400,000 tons of octopuses were caught for food in 2015. Octopuses are also harvested as bait for catching fish. Even when they aren't targeted, octopuses can get caught in fishing nets. And certain types of fishing damage their habitats.

▶ Vendors sell octopuses as food in South Korea.

36

Inspired by Octopuses

Octopuses have survived so long thanks to many ingenious **adaptations**. Scientists are studying the animals to learn how their brains and bodies work. Research findings are inspiring new technology to help people.

Engineers are trying to make materials that imitate an octopus's camouflaging skill. In 2014, a team in Illinois created a flexible grid filled with dye that can change colors. **Sensors** in the bottom layer detect what's under the grid. The top layer turns black or white to match what the sensors see. Eventually, this technology could be used to develop color-changing clothing. People like soldiers could use it to blend in with their surroundings.

Engineers in Massachusetts have developed a robot called the octobot. Most robots have metal joints and other hard parts. But like the animal it is named for, the octobot's body is soft. Liquid flows through tubes in the robot's body to move it. One day, similar soft robots could help people explore small spaces or even perform surgery.

◄ Engineers modeled this robot gripper after an octopus's arm.

Clever Creatures

Octopuses are popular attractions in aquariums worldwide. To keep the smart animals busy, keepers give them puzzles. They hide food inside sealed jars that the octopuses unscrew. One aquarium even gave an octopus meals in a childproof pill bottle. The octopus learned to open the bottle in less than five minutes!

Not surpisingly, octopuses aren't easy to keep in **captivity**. They sometimes use their intelligence and flexibility to escape. In 2016, an octopus named Inky disappeared from a New Zealand aquarium. He squeezed through a tiny valve to leave his tank. Then he seemingly scooted 8 ft. (2.4 m) across the floor, wiggled down a drainpipe, and was never seen again!

People were intrigued by Inky's story. They tried to imagine what the octopus thought as he made his escape. Over the years, scientists have learned a lot about octopuses. But there are some secrets these clever creatures will always keep to themselves.

▶ An octopus pulls a cork out of a glass jar to reach the shrimp inside.

Octopus Family Tree

Octopuses and other cephalopods are mollusks—animals with soft, boneless bodies; muscular mantles; and raspy tongues. All mollusks have a common ancestor that lived more than 500 million years ago. This diagram shows how octopuses are related to other mollusks, such as squid, clams, and snails. The closer together two animals are on the tree, the more alike they are.

Nautiluses
cephalopods that have spiral shells and simple eyes and that swim backward by shooting out water

Sea Slugs
colorful mollusks that lack shells and that live underwater and breathe through gills

Clams
headless underwater mollusks with hinged shells that clasp shut for protection

Land Snails
air-breathing mollusks with hard shells, tentacles, and slimy mucus to keep them from drying out

Ancestor of all Mollusks

Note: Animal photos are not to scale.

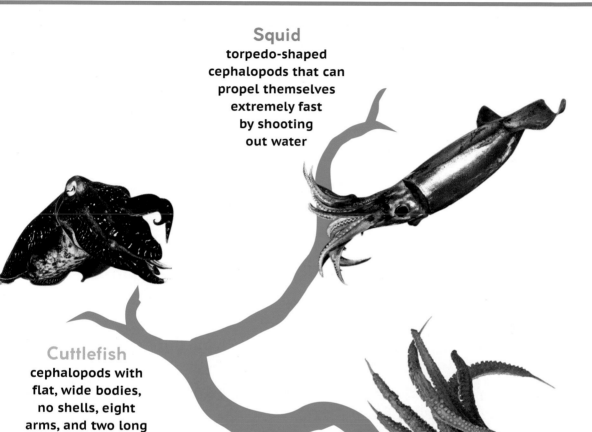

Squid
torpedo-shaped
cephalopods that can
propel themselves
extremely fast
by shooting
out water

Cuttlefish
cephalopods with
flat, wide bodies,
no shells, eight
arms, and two long
tentacles

Octopuses
cephalopods with eight
long arms, no fins or
shells, and ink sacs;
tend to live on the
seafloor

Words to Know

A .... **adaptations** *(ad-ap-TAY-shuns)* changes a living thing goes through so it fits in better within its environment

ancestors *(ANN-sess-turs)* family members who lived long ago

C .... **camouflage** *(KAM-uh-flahzh)* a way of hiding by using coloring, pattern, or shape to blend into one's surroundings

captivity *(kap-TIV-i-tee)* the condition of living in the care of people

carnivores *(KAHR-nuh-vorz)* animals that eat meat

chromatophores *(kro-MAT-uh-forz)* colored cells in the skin of an animal

D .... **dens** *(DENZ)* the homes of wild animals

E .... **ecosystem** *(EE-koh-sis-tuhm)* all the living things in a place and their relation to their environment

embryos *(EM-bree-ohz)* the earliest forms of unborn humans or animals

exoskeleton *(ex-oh-SKEL-uh-tuhn)* the hard outer covering of invertebrate animals such as lobsters, crabs, and insects

F .... **forage** *(FOR-ij)* to go in search of food

fossils *(FAH-suhls)* bones, shells, or other traces of animals or plants from millions of years ago, preserved as rock

H .... **habitat** *(HAB-i-tat)* the place where an animal or plant is usually found

I .... **invertebrates** *(in-VUHR-tuh-brits)* animals without a backbone

M .... **mammals** *(MAM-uhlz)* warm-blooded animals that have hair or fur and usually give birth to live babies; female mammals produce milk to feed their young

mate *(MAYT)* to come together to produce young

N .... **nocturnal** *(nahk-TUR-nuhl)* active at night

P .... **plankton** *(PLANK-tuhn)* tiny plants and animals that float or drift in ocean water

predators *(PRED-uh-tuhrs)* animals that live by hunting other animals for food

prey *(PRAY)* an animal that is hunted by another animal for food

S .... **scavengers** *(SKAV-uhn-jerz)* animals that eat dead and decaying material

sensors *(SEN-surz)* instruments that can detect and measure changes and transmit the information to a controlling device

solitary *(SAH-li-ter-ee)* not requiring or without the companionship of others

species *(SPEE-sheez)* one of the groups into which animals and plants are divided; members of the same species can mate and have offspring

V .... **venom** *(VEN-um)* a poison made by some animals that is injected into prey usually by biting or stinging

Find Out More

BOOKS

- Claybourne, Anna. *Octopuses* (Animal Abilities). Chicago: Capstone Raintree, 2013.

- Gish, Melissa. *Octopuses* (Living Wild). Mankato, MN: Creative Company, 2014.

- Montgomery, Sy. *The Octopus Scientists: Exploring the Mind of a Mollusk* (Scientists in the Field). New York: Houghton Mifflin Harcourt, 2015.

- Rice, Dona Herweck. *Color-Changing Cephalopods* (Smithsonian STEAM Readers). Huntington Beach, CA: Teacher Created Materials Publishing, 2018.

- Riggs, Kate. *Octopuses* (Amazing Animals). Mankato, MN: Creative Company, 2016.

To find more books and resources about animals, visit:
scholastic.com

Index

Index (continued)

About the Author

Mara Grunbaum is a science writer in Seattle,
Washington. She loves to learn about all kinds of
animals—but especially the really weird ones.
She lives with her cat, Zadie, and likes to visit the
Seattle Aquarium, where the resident giant Pacific
octopus is always doing something sneaky.